to

....

from

....

date

....

Praise for *When God Says, "Go"*

"Few books have stilled my soul and shifted my faith perspective like *When God Says 'Go'*. Elizabeth's vast knowledge of scripture, her invitation to explore the stories of biblical men and women, and her encouragement to saturate ourselves in truth rather than circumstance is powerfully transformative. If you're looking for a deep dive into the reminder that God is always with you, *When God Says 'Go'* will be your new favorite resource and study guide."

–Bekah Jane Pogue, author of *Choosing REAL,* national speaker, writing & speaking coach, Encouraging Soul Care at bekahpogue.com

"Elizabeth Laing Thompson holds your hand, dismisses your excuses, gives you fuel for the race, and empowers you to take that first walk on the waves in *When God Says 'Go'*. Be inspired by her authentic, friendly voice and her biblical arsenal. You're not alone. She has stood where you stand, and she jumped. This book of faith will help you jump too."

–Andy Lee, author of *A Mary Like Me: Flawed Yet Called* and
The Book of Ruth Key Word Bible Study:
A 31-Day Journey to Hope and Promise

"*Did God just really ask this of me? So now what? Why me? How can I possibly do what God is asking?* A relatable and biblically sound book, *When God Says 'Go'* addresses the hang-ups and hiccups honest Christians face as they live out their faith. Elizabeth's encouragement and wisdom are sure to turn chronic freaker-outers into confident, faithful followers of the God who continues to say, *Go!*"

–Tracy Steel, recovering freaker-outer, speaker,
and writer at www.tracymsteel.com.

"*When God Says 'Go'* gives us the gentle nudge and the affirmed push to step into who God is calling us to be. Elizabeth explains that road may not always be easy, but neither has it been easy for anyone God has drawn into a meaningful calling. I'm so grateful for Elizabeth's words, for the way she both encourages us to be bold and nourishes our hearts with her writing. I highly recommend this book for any woman looking down the individually incredible path God has set for each of us."

–Emily Ley, author of *A Simplified Life*

"Elizabeth is an absolute marvel. She writes in a style that is witty, relatable, and downright fun to read. In *When God Says 'Go'*, Elizabeth bridges time and helps us connect with biblical characters from long-ago. They become contemporary friends instead of ancient acquaintances. We feel as if we are right there with them as they wrestle with feelings of fear, unease, and confusion while listening to God's call of, *Go!* This book is a must-read for anyone not quite certain of how to proceed when God calls us forward. Isn't that all of us? As Elizabeth says, 'God is calling us all to go somewhere new in our walk with Him.' I am so relieved that Elizabeth helps and encourages us to rise to the challenge. She is our trusty trail-guide whose wisdom we are all fortunate to heed."

–Sarah Philpott, author of *Loved Baby: 31 Devotions Helping You Grieve and Cherish Your Child after Pregnancy Loss*

"When I was young, it was pretty easy to pick up and go when God called. After all, my only real possessions were a TV and four cinder blocks to hold it up! Things are a bit different these days with a full family and growing business: "going" has gotten quite a bit harder! I found Elizabeth's book to be incredibly timely for me. She gives real, practical, and theologically sound advice in a very digestible format. I love the example narratives that pull you into the biblical stories and her own personal experiences. These helped tremendously in applying the truths of the book. I'd recommend this book to anyone who is serious about pursuing God no matter where He may lead."

–Spence Hackney, President and Creative Director,
Proclaim Interactive

"*When God Says 'Go'* offered poignant and heartfelt reminders about our unique opportunities to serve God and how to peacefully trust His ways. Elizabeth's beautifully told stories reignited my heart and commitment for going all in for Jesus. Whether it requires a huge transformation or a 'yes' right where we are, giving God our all is truly the best way to live. This book will challenge you, convict you, make you chuckle, and leave you wiping tears before you close the last page."

–Courtney Westlake, author of *A Different Beautiful*

"If you are hesitant about what God has called you to do, *When God Says 'Go'* is a must-read book that will transform your fear into courage. Elizabeth Laing Thompson breaks down biblical examples of scripture in a way that will leave you wanting to read more. This book will encourage you to boldly answer God's call on your life with confidence and expectation—to courageously say yes when God says go."

–Caroline Harries, author of *In Due Time*, blogger

Elizabeth Laing Thompson

When God Says

Says

A Devotional Thought Journal

SHILOH RUN PRESS
An Imprint of Barbour Publishing, Inc.

© 2020 by Elizabeth Laing Thompson

ISBN 978-1-64352-360-6

Published by Shiloh Run Press, an imprint of Barbour Publishing, Inc., 1810 Barbour Drive, Uhrichsville, Ohio 44683, www.shilohrunpress.com

Our mission is to inspire the world with the life-changing message of the Bible.

Member of the
Evangelical Christian
Publishers Association

Printed in China.

go: the smallest of words, the biggest of meanings. . .

It might be one of God's favorite words.

Sometimes life is calm. Secure. Peaceful. Nothing scary, each day much like the one before. That's usually when God shows up. That's usually when God says, "Go."

Sometimes God calls dramatically, in miracle and flame. Sometimes He calls subtly, in stillness and whisper, so soft we won't hear if we aren't listening. Sometimes through His Word, sometimes through a friend, sometimes through life events.

However He speaks, God calls to us all. We are called for different roles, in different ways, at different points in our lives: one season holds one purpose, the next holds another. We are God's people, His instruments, and He wants to use us. As Romans 8:28 puts it, "We know that in all things God works for the good of those who love him, who have been called according to his purpose." *According to His purpose.* God has plans for each of us. He has work for us to do, work He prepared a long time ago, work He has equipped us to accomplish: "For we are God's handiwork, created in Christ Jesus to do good works, which God prepared in advance for us to do" (Ephesians 2:10).

God is calling. . . . Will we answer His call?

~Elizabeth

He has saved us and called us to a holy life—
not because of anything we have done but because
of his own purpose and grace. This grace was given us
in Christ Jesus before the beginning of time.
2 TIMOTHY 1:9

The question isn't *Is God calling?*, because God is always calling. Always urging us onward, giving us purpose, encouraging us to grow. The question is *Will we answer His call?*

Maybe it's time to go. Go somewhere new, someplace we've never been. A geographical place, a spiritual place, a relational place. Maybe it's time to move forward after being stuck with one foot in the past. Or time to go deeper—in Bible study or intimacy. Time to go higher—in prayer or in dreams.

Maybe it's time to give: to use talents and opportunities God has given.

Or maybe it's time to grow, right where we are: to dig into the Word, dive into our heart, and become the person God is calling us to be.

As you begin this journal, take a moment to reflect and write: How are you feeling called (or maybe pushed or prodded!) by God? How are your confidence, your courage, and your mood? Where is your faith? Now write down where you would like to be: Who do you hope to become as you pray your way through these pages? In what ways do you want to grow? Pray through the things you have written down.

....

....

....

....

....

....

....

....

....

When God says, "Go," we face a choice. Will we swallow hard and step up, saying, "Here am I. Send me!"? Or will we sit back and stay safe, stammering, "But Lord. . ."? Whether we're ready or not, God is calling us all to go somewhere new in our walk with Him. So what are we waiting for? Let's answer His call. Let's go for it.

Which call feels the most relevant to your life right now: move (move somewhere new, redirect your life in some way), give (give more to God or to people), or grow (face a weakness, develop a new strength)?

....

....

....

....

....

....

....

....

....

....

....

....

"So now, go. I am sending you to Pharaoh to bring my people the Israelites out of Egypt." But Moses said to God, "Who am I that I should go to Pharaoh and bring the Israelites out of Egypt?" And God said, "I will be with you."

Exodus 3:10–12

When God calls you, it's not about you—it's about Him. God's call isn't about our age, our experience, our qualifications, our giftedness, our skill set, our appearance, our intelligence, our education, our heritage, our connections, our bank balance, our college transcript, our curriculum vitae, our marital status, our family background, our track record, our level of influence, our social media following. Nor is it about our character traits—courage, integrity, wisdom. Nor is it about our spiritual résumé—faith level, failures, triumphs.

God's call is about God. It is about God being with His people. And guess what? God was—as He still is and always will be—fully qualified.

How does it make you feel to realize God's call is not about you, but about Him? If you embrace this perspective, how will it change your view of whatever challenge lies before you?

....

....

....

....

....

....

....

....

....

....

....

· ·

For who is God except the LORD? Who but our God is a solid rock?
God arms me with strength, and he makes my way perfect.
He makes me as surefooted as a deer, enabling me to stand on
mountain heights. He trains my hands for battle; he strengthens
my arm to draw a bronze bow. You have given me your shield
of victory. Your right hand supports me; your help has
made me great. You have made a wide path
for my feet to keep them from slipping.
PSALM 18:31–36 NLT

· ·

God is old enough. Wise enough. Smart enough. Rich enough. Experienced enough. Educated enough. Influential enough. Successful enough. Righteous enough. Confident enough. Brave enough.

It didn't matter if Jeremiah, Moses, Gideon—or any of the people God called in the pages of scripture—were qualified, because God was with them, and that was the only qualification they needed. When God is with you, you are qualified for your call. When God is with you, you have all you need.

How does your perspective change if you truly believe God is with you, and He is fully qualified? How do you see God with you even now?

....

....

....

....

....

....

....

....

....

....

....

....

*"The Lord your God, who is going before you,
will fight for you, as he did for you in Egypt, before
your very eyes, and in the wilderness. There you saw how
the Lord your God carried you, as a father carries his son,
all the way you went until you reached this place."*

DEUTERONOMY 1:30-31

G od won't just say, "Ready, set, go!"—and then abandon you half-way through the race. He will see you through the part where legs grow tired and lungs scream for mercy. He will see you all the way to the finish line.

Try this: Find a psalm to serve as a theme psalm for this time in your life—perhaps it describes how you feel about whatever challenges you are facing; perhaps it gives you the words you need to pray. Try reading it in several Bible versions to give you a fuller understanding of its meaning. Write your psalm in the space below, and pray through your psalm every day this week. There are many ways to pray through a psalm: You can simply read it to God. You can also read a verse or two, pause to add your own thoughts, then read the next verse, and so on, all the way to the end.

....

....

....

....

....

....

....

....

....

In all my prayers for all of you, I always pray with joy because of your partnership in the gospel from the first day until now, being confident of this, that he who began a good work in you will carry it on to completion until the day of Christ Jesus.

PHILIPPIANS 1:4–6

Can you imagine losing the chains of insecurity that have kept you bound for so long? No longer feeling hampered by your own limitations or held back by the fear of what others think? When we live our life devoted to fulfilling God's purposes, we stop worrying about ourselves: our success, our reputation, our appearance. We lose ourselves in Him. In His purpose. In His call. We seek only to hear those blessed words at life's end: "Well done, good and faithful servant!" (Matthew 25:21).

Write about a time when you have thought, "Maybe God wants me to. . . ," but then you held back because you were afraid or lacked confidence. Now write about a time when you set fear and insecurity aside in order to respond to God's call. What made the difference?

I prayed to the Lord, and he answered me. He freed me from all my fears. Those who look to him for help will be radiant with joy; no shadow of shame will darken their faces. In my desperation I prayed, and the Lord listened; he saved me from all my troubles.

PSALM 34:4–6 NLT

Being called by God doesn't come with the promise, "And then everything will be easy and perfect and you'll live happily ever after!" Nope. Fulfilling God's call may be challenging—maybe even the most challenging thing we've ever faced. But we can face it, we can rise to meet it, we can cross that finish line. With God's help, we can see His call to completion.

When God calls us to something new, instead of saying, "But Lord, I (insert fear, insecurity, limitation, excuse, or objection here)," we get to say, "But God can." Create your list of "But God can. . ." statements in the journaling space below.

....

....

....

....

....

....

....

....

....

....

....

....

● ●

"Before I formed you in the womb I knew you, before you were born I set you apart; I appointed you as a prophet to the nations."

·JEREMIAH 1:5

● ●

God called you before you were born. God has purposes for you. Good works for you to perform. Roles and responsibilities for you to fulfill. He's been planning them for a long time. Setting them up for you. Moving things around to get them ready. And on the day you were born, I picture Him watching from heaven, cheering and rubbing His almighty hands together and saying to Jesus, "I've been waiting for this one. She's got a lot I need her to do. Now we can get started."

Describe a time when you had an "aha" moment when you realized: "God gave me this experience or gift or personality trait for a reason! He is using it for His purposes even now!"

....

....

....

....

....

....

....

....

....

....

....

....

Thus he shows for all time the tremendous generosity of the grace and kindness he has expressed towards us in Christ Jesus. It was nothing you could or did achieve—it was God's gift to you. No one can pride himself upon earning the love of God. The fact is that what we are we owe to the hand of God upon us. We are born afresh in Christ, and born to do those good deeds which God planned for us to do.

EPHESIANS 2:8-10 PHILLIPS

When God calls you to fulfill a "good work" He has in mind for your life, you may not have all the qualities and qualifications you need, but God does. And when God calls you, you can be sure of this: You have been prequalified. He Himself will put up whatever you need to help you fulfill your part. God Himself is investing in your future. What you lack, He will loan. What you need, He will provide.

Fill in the blank: "Ah, Lord, I am too _____ (weak, scared, old, young, sinful, proud, angry, uneducated, broken. . .)" Can you find a scripture to help you view that "limitation" from God's perspective? Write it down here.

....

....

....

....

....

....

....

....

....

....

....

For those God foreknew he also predestined to be conformed to the image of his Son, that he might be the firstborn among many brothers and sisters. And those he predestined, he also called; those he called, he also justified; those he justified, he also glorified.

ROMANS 8:29-30

Here's a truth we have to embrace if we ever want to heal—from fear, from hurt, from sin, from any kind of brokenness: God chose us *because of our weakness*.

Foolish. Powerless. Despised. Counted as nothing. If you have ever felt like those words describe you, then first, welcome to the We're All Unworthy Club, and second, rejoice in knowing that your weakness brings all the more glory to God!

How might God want to use your broken places for His purposes—to help a hurting person, to strengthen your character, to prepare you for service?

....

....

....

....

....

....

....

....

....

....

....

....

*His divine power has given us everything we need
for a godly life through our knowledge of him
who called us by his own glory and goodness.*

2 PETER 1:3

God gives His salvation and affection freely and lavishly, and they were paid for—fully paid for—by the blood of Christ. But even so, once we are saved, we all have work to do. Our Maker created us to crave purpose and meaning, and He has assigned us each a set of tasks and roles that will give us that fulfillment—and serve His purposes along the way.

Journal an answer to this question (and have fun—don't be afraid to dream!): What specific purposes do you think God has in mind for your life as a whole? What new purposes might He have in mind for your current season of life?

....

....

....

....

....

....

....

....

....

....

....

....

Remember, dear brothers and sisters, that few of you were wise in the world's eyes or powerful or wealthy when God called you. Instead, God chose things the world considers foolish in order to shame those who think they are wise. And he chose things that are powerless to shame those who are powerful. God chose things despised by the world, things counted as nothing at all, and used them to bring to nothing what the world considers important. As a result, no one can ever boast in the presence of God.

1 CORINTHIANS 1:26–29 NLT

If you struggle with believing lies about your forgiveness and worthiness, write them down and speak them aloud to God and to a godly friend. Lies lose power when they escape our heads and are exposed to the light of day—more, to the light of Christ. (See John 3:19–21.)

List the lies you struggle with on a daily basis. Then list the truth according to God's Word.

....

....

....

....

....

....

....

....

....

....

....

....

....

....

Then I heard a loud voice in heaven say: "Now have come the salvation and the power and the kingdom of our God, and the authority of his Messiah. For the accuser of our brothers and sisters, who accuses them before our God day and night, has been hurled down."

REVELATION 12:10

Blameless means no guilt. No shame. No regret. Now tell me, is that how you feel? Because it's how Christians should feel! And get this—*it's how our loving Father wants us to feel*. He spent millennia and gave His Son's life in purchasing this expensive gift, this lavish gift, for us; let us not now despise the gift by refusing it. By devaluing it. By saying, "Thanks, but no thanks. I can't accept this. Don't You know I'm not worthy?"

Journal answers to some of these questions:
If you allowed yourself to fully enjoy the grace of God, to completely escape the shackles of guilt and shame and regret,
- *how would you feel about yourself?*
- *what kind of friend would you be?*
- *how would you perform at school or at work?*
- *how would you relate to your loved ones?*
- *how would you share your faith?*

Now pray about what you have written, asking God to help you embrace His grace. Step into the light and enjoy your Father's wondrous gift!

....

....

....

....

....

....

....

....

....

Jesus replied, "Very truly I tell you, everyone who sins is a slave
to sin. Now a slave has no permanent place in the family,
but a son belongs to it forever. So if the Son
sets you free, you will be free indeed."

JOHN 8:34–36

_____

_____

_____

_____

_____

_____

_____

_____

_____

_____

_____

_____

_____

_____

_____

_____

Of course we're not worthy! *No one is.* Our unworthiness is the whole point. Let us not allow God's generous grace to go to waste. Yes, it is precious and priceless, and no, we don't deserve it—but let us accept and enjoy it. Grace is a gift and it is fully ours.

Try this: Begin creating a playlist of spiritual songs that put you in touch with God's gracious love and help you find courage and confidence in Him. Write down some of your favorite lyrics here.

For he chose us in him before the creation of the world to be holy and blameless in his sight. In love he predestined us for adoption to sonship through Jesus Christ, in accordance with his pleasure and will—to the praise of his glorious grace, which he has freely given us in the One he loves. In him we have redemption through his blood, the forgiveness of sins, in accordance with the riches of God's grace that he lavished on us.

EPHESIANS 1:4–8

Sometimes we act as though God is not omniscient. As though we have been sly enough to outsmart Him, sneaky enough to weasel our way into His kingdom. We worry that if He ever found out how terrible we are—how sinful our past, how dark our darkness—He would immediately send the angel police to arrest us and kick us out for trespassing in His kingdom! My friend, God saved you even knowing how sinful you are—and the truth is, He grasps the heartache, the ugliness, and the pain caused by your sins even more than you do. And *even so*, He wants to save you. *Even so*, He offers His Son's pure blood on your behalf. This is amazing grace indeed.

God knows everything about you. Every. Thing. And even so, He loves you. Write a prayer of thanksgiving, telling Him how His grace makes you feel.

....

....

....

....

....

....

....

....

....

....

Therefore, since we have a great high priest who has ascended into heaven, Jesus the Son of God, let us hold firmly to the faith we profess. For we do not have a high priest who is unable to empathize with our weaknesses, but we have one who has been tempted in every way, just as we are—yet he did not sin. Let us then approach God's throne of grace with confidence, so that we may receive mercy and find grace to help us in our time of need.

HEBREWS 4:14-16

Don't let shame keep you from going where God wants you to go. From becoming the person He has already empowered you to become.

What would change if you truly felt no shame? If you embraced God's gift of blamelessness? How would you. . .think differently? Carry yourself? Change in your closest relationships?

....

....

....

....

....

....

....

....

....

....

....

....

....

....

*Oh, what joy for those whose disobedience is forgiven, whose sin
is put out of sight! Yes, what joy for those whose record the L*ORD
*has cleared of guilt, whose lives are lived in complete honesty! . . .
Finally, I confessed all my sins to you and stopped trying to
hide my guilt. I said to myself, "I will confess my rebellion
to the L*ORD*." And you forgave me! All my guilt is gone.*

P SALM 32:1-2, 5 NLT

*D*on't let regret keep you from moving forward. Don't let lingering feelings of guilt—feelings that are just feelings, and not reality—keep you stuck in the past. Maybe God's call to you is, "Go! Leave your past in the past and move forward with your life. Take the gift of grace I have offered you and run with it!"

Have you already seen God use your weakness, sins, and brokenness for His good purposes? How might God want to use those things in the future?

....

....

....

....

....

....

....

....

....

....

....

....

....

....

"Forget the former things; do not dwell on the past. See, I am doing a new thing! Now it springs up; do you not perceive it? I am making a way in the wilderness and streams in the wasteland."

ISAIAH 43:18–19

D*on't let shame silence you.* You have a testimony—perhaps it's a messy one, filled with embarrassing stories and an R-rated past, not suitable for young audiences. . .but what glory your transformation can bring to the name of Christ! What praise He can receive through you and your mess!

Describe your testimony of transformation here.

....

....

....

....

....

....

....

....

....

....

....

....

....

....

"I will give you back your health and heal your wounds,"
says the LORD. "For you are called an outcast—
'Jerusalem for whom no one cares.' "

JEREMIAH 30:17 NLT

The more difficult your past, the greater your miracle. The more you have been forgiven, the more grace you have to give. The Lord did not save you just for you. He saved you for others. So that you might go. Go with your scars, go as you heal, go and tell. Go be the light He left burning here on earth.

Who might be encouraged to hear your story? Which of your scars might help someone else to find healing?

....

....

....

....

....

....

....

....

....

....

....

....

....

....

"If you want to be my disciple, you must, by comparison, hate everyone else—your father and mother, wife and children, brothers and sisters—yes, even your own life. Otherwise, you cannot be my disciple. And if you do not carry your own cross and follow me, you cannot be my disciple."

LUKE 14:26-27 NLT

It's an unflinching standard. Coming to Jesus costs everything: relationships, possessions, talents. Jesus calls us to put Him first. And not just first—He wants to be first, last, and everything in between. He wants to *be* our life. As Paul put it, "Christ. . .is your life" (Colossians 3:4).

What scares you most about giving your all to Jesus? About going overboard for Him?

"And be sure of this: I am with you always, even to the end of the age."

<small>MATTHEW 28:20 NLT</small>

Yes, the older we get the more we have to lose. Yes, we know more than we wish we did about the ways of the world, the pain in the world. But no matter our age or stage of life, the *same Jesus* is out there waiting for us. The *same Jesus* is ready to catch us if the wind and waves get the better of us. He is just as faithful, just as trustworthy, just as powerful now as He was when we first tried our hands—or rather our feet—at water-walking.

How has God remained faithful to you through the years? How has He proven Himself trustworthy? List as many specific moments of His faithfulness as you can fit on this page. (And hey—no one's going to stop you from spilling over onto more pages if you've got a thousand examples!)

....

....

....

....

....

....

....

....

....

....

....

....

"Today I have given you the choice between life and death, between blessings and curses. Now I call on heaven and earth to witness the choice you make. Oh, that you would choose life, so that you and your descendants might live! You can make this choice by loving the LORD your God, obeying him, and committing yourself firmly to him. This is the key to your life. And if you love and obey the LORD, you will live long in the land the LORD swore to give your ancestors Abraham, Isaac, and Jacob."

DEUTERONOMY 30:19-20 NLT

A come-to-Jesus is a point in time when life stops for one fleeting *Matrix* moment: Time slows. Fog clears. Vision sharpens. Here in one standing-on-the-ledge moment, we have an opportunity to change. To confront ourselves, demons and all; to stare the truest, most sinful, ugliest parts of our sinful nature square in the face. To behold grace in all its beauty, held out for us even here in this dark moment, ready for the taking—and then to give our all to Jesus. To give *ourselves* to Jesus. To say, "Here I am, Lord. I surrender. Take me and change me. I'm Yours."

The Bible calls this repentance.

Have you ever gone "all in" for Jesus? If not, what will it take to make that all-important decision, and what spiritual friend(s) can support and encourage you along the way?

Shortly before dawn Jesus went out to them, walking on the lake. When the disciples saw him walking on the lake, they were terrified. "It's a ghost," they said, and cried out in fear. But Jesus immediately said to them: "Take courage! It is I. Don't be afraid." "Lord, if it's you," Peter replied, "tell me to come to you on the water." "Come," he said. Then Peter got down out of the boat, walked on the water and came toward Jesus. But when he saw the wind, he was afraid and, beginning to sink, cried out, "Lord, save me!" Immediately Jesus reached out his hand and caught him. "You of little faith," he said, "why did you doubt?"

MATTHEW 14:25–31

If I were Peter on that stormy night, I might have been tempted to say, "You know, Jesus, I am excited about the opportunity to walk on water with You. Truly, I am. But couldn't You do that trick where You calm the wind and waves first? You know, the miracle You did that time when You were napping on the boat and we were all freaking out? (Not our finest hour, I know.) I think the walk would be so much more enjoyable for both of us if the water were calm, don't You? Not to mention a little less scary and dangerous? Don't You think the whole water-walking concept is radical enough without the complication of the crazy waves?"

Anybody else like to negotiate with God like this? Manipulate circumstances to remove as much risk and discomfort as possible? But when I—can I say we?—try to negotiate with God like this, how much we miss! We miss the excitement of adventure, the exhilaration of trust, the mind-blowing miracle of "This is all God and no me—this could only happen with Him."

If you could negotiate with God to make His calling easier, what kinds of things would you say? How would you change His calls for your life?

....

....

....

....

....

....

....

....

....

And let us run with perseverance the race marked out for us, fixing our eyes on Jesus, the pioneer and perfecter of faith. For the joy set before him he endured the cross, scorning its shame, and sat down at the right hand of the throne of God. Consider him who endured such opposition from sinners, so that you will not grow weary and lose heart.
HEBREWS 12:1–3

When Jesus says, "Come," we have to get out of our safe, comfortable boat with its life rafts and ropes, and we have to walk on water. We have to go out where it's dangerous. Out where no one but Jesus can help us walk. Out where we cannot survive on our own. Out where other believers might not dare to go. And if we don't want to sink, we have to take our eyes off the wind and the waves and fix them on Jesus.

If you have gone all in in the past but have since taken some steps back, can you identify an area in which you want to go all in again? What will it take for you to make that decision? Pray about it, describing your fears and hesitations to God and asking Him to give you the strength to jump out of the boat.

....

....

....

....

....

....

....

....

....

....

....

....

I was right on the cliff-edge, ready to fall, when GOD grabbed and held me. GOD's my strength, he's also my song, and now he's my salvation. Hear the shouts, hear the triumph songs in the camp of the saved? "The hand of GOD has turned the tide! The hand of GOD is raised in victory! The hand of GOD has turned the tide!"

PSALM 118:13–16 MSG

Jesus calls us all, no matter where we are: New to faith, pondering a jump. Settled in Christ, needing a push. Mature in Christ, fighting weariness. At every stage, God calls us forward. At every age, Jesus says, "Come." He stands before us, arms wide, promising that if we jump—when we jump—though the waves may be wild, our feet will stand firm.

Push yourself to exercise fresh courage this week—to take one simple step forward in one area of life. Perhaps that means introducing yourself to a new person at school or work, or sharing your faith with a neighbor or friend. Perhaps it means speaking up when your feelings get hurt. Perhaps it means applying for a promotion—or simply brushing up your résumé in preparation for applying. Write down some ideas here, and pray about them.

....

....

....

....

....

....

....

....

....

....

*God is faithful, who has called you into fellowship
with his Son, Jesus Christ our Lord.*

1 CORINTHIANS 1:9

Jesus loves us and gives us grace when we fall short. When He calls us to come, He doesn't just challenge us; He also comforts us. Walks alongside us. Protects us. Heals us. He promises, "Come to Me, all you who are weary, and I will give you rest. My yoke is easy and My burden is light" (see Matthew 11:28–30). And He says, "I have come that they may have life, and have it to the full" (John 10:10). Somehow the difficult things and the comforting things are all true—equally true—at the same time. This is one of the deep mysteries of our faith. A beautiful paradox.

Describe a scary or difficult time in your life when you felt or saw God's hand at work. How specifically did He care for you, comfort you, protect you, or spare you?

....

....

....

....

....

....

....

....

....

....

....

*Grace to all who love our Lord Jesus
Christ with an undying love.*
EPHESIANS 6:24

Let's not overthink our Christianity any more than we overthink our commitments in marriage. We have to count the cost, yes; we're called to go all in, yes; but let's remember: We get married because we're in love. We get married because we have found our favorite person. We are willing to do the hard stuff because all the good stuff is *so totally worth it*. It's the same with Christianity. We go all in for Jesus because we love Him. We go all in for Jesus because He is the greatest person ever in the history of people. We go all in for Jesus because He went all in for us first. We go all in for Jesus because He shows us how we were meant to live, who we were meant to be.

List the reasons you are all in for Jesus.

....

....

....

....

....

....

....

....

....

....

....

"I know your deeds, your hard work and your perseverance. . . .
You have persevered and have endured hardships for my name,
and have not grown weary. Yet I hold this against you: You
have forsaken the love you had at first. Consider how far you
have fallen! Repent and do the things you did at first."
REVELATION 2:2, 3-5

Maybe you have gone all in for Jesus in the past, but as life has changed, you also have changed; you have taken some steps back. What would it look like if you went all in for Jesus now? At *this* stage of your life? Now as a college student. . .a married woman. . .a working woman. . .a divorcée. . .a parent. . .a grandparent?

What is different about going all in for Jesus at this point in your life than when you first started following Him? Do you find that it is easier or more difficult to go all in for Jesus the older you get? Why?

....

....

....

....

....

....

....

....

....

....

....

....

....

....

"I myself said, 'How gladly would I treat you like my children and give you a pleasant land, the most beautiful inheritance of any nation.' I thought you would call me 'Father' and not turn away from following me."

JEREMIAH 3:19

Christianity isn't a list of "to dos" and "to give ups." No, Christianity is a *relationship*. A choice to give ourselves wholly to the One who loves us and wants our love in return. The One who keeps seeking us, meeting our crossed arms with His open ones.

How do you feel differently about God's call when you focus on relationship instead of rules?

....

....

....

....

....

....

....

....

....

....

....

....

....

....

....

"The kingdom of heaven is like treasure hidden in a field. When a man found it, he hid it again, and then in his joy went and sold all he had and bought that field. Again, the kingdom of heaven is like a merchant looking for fine pearls. When he found one of great value, he went away and sold everything he had and bought it."

MATTHEW 13:44–46

Yes, the price of following Jesus is scary, overwhelming, and expensive, but it would be wrong for us to water down His call to make it easier or more palatable. As my preacher father likes to say, "The pearl of great price never goes on sale"—and it's worth every penny.

How did you feel when you first found God? What were you most grateful for?

And as we live in God, our love grows more perfect. So we will not be afraid on the day of judgment, but we can face him with confidence because we live like Jesus here in this world. Such love has no fear, because perfect love expels all fear. If we are afraid, it is for fear of punishment, and this shows that we have not fully experienced his perfect love. We love each other because he loved us first.

1 JOHN 4:17–19 NLT

If it's time for you to change—if God is forcing your hand and you can't stay the same—know this: God is love, and love gives strength. Love conquers fear.

How does love help you—and sometimes force you—to conquer fear?

....

....

....

....

....

....

....

....

....

....

....

....

....

....

....

Listen to me, you islands; hear this, you distant nations:
Before I was born the L<small>ORD</small> *called me; from my*
mother's womb he has spoken my name.

I<small>SAIAH</small> 49:1

We cannot run from crisis situations. Some are griefs that feel past bearing, past surviving—and yet we must bear them. We must survive them. The only way out is through. And in situations like this, God is saying, "Grow." He gives us no choice but to move forward. No choice but to change.

Why might God sometimes deliver us through difficult situations rather than from difficult situations? (In other words, why doesn't God always take away difficulties when we ask Him to?)

*"I am the L*ORD*; that is my name! I will not yield my glory to another or my praise to idols. See, the former things have taken place, and new things I declare; before they spring into being I announce them to you." Sing to the L*ORD *a new song, his praise from the ends of the earth.*

ISAIAH 42:8-10

While most of us won't receive an angelic visit announcing our next life surprise, we all experience change: moves, promotions, job loss, marriage, infertility, pregnancy, health problems, conflict, financial struggle. . .and the list goes on. Even when our life changes come from a "human," earthbound source, we can be sure that God is not unaware—or uninvolved in our journey.

Pay attention to little encouragements God sends you each day to show you His presence and love and to ease the pain of whatever difficulties you are facing. (We're talking about small things here: a card in the mail, free lunch for no reason, even getting that parking space you prayed for!) Spend this week writing down your "God moments" every night before you go to bed, and thank God for them again the next morning. Keep your list on this page.

....

....

....

....

....

....

....

....

....

....

....

....

"I will lead the blind by ways they have not known, along unfamiliar paths I will guide them; I will turn the darkness into light before them and make the rough places smooth. These are the things I will do; I will not forsake them."

Isaiah 42:16

Has God ever changed your life plan? Pushed you to go in a new and unexpected direction? A direction you might not have chosen for yourself?

Here's how it usually goes when God hands me a life change I hadn't anticipated:

God: *So guess what? Some things are about to change in your life. It's time to go in a new direction. It's time for something different.*

Me *(crazy eyed and squeaky voiced)*: *Different? What do you mean, different? As long as different means "basically the exact same way life has been," then that's totally fine. I'm completely up for it. I trust You. . . .*

(Long, quiet pause. God raises an eyebrow, looking vaguely amused. . . .)

Me *(breathing fast, riffling through cabinets, searching for a paper bag)*: *Sorry, one more thing. As long as different means "exactly what I had planned for my life, only a slightly happier and more successful plan than I had dared to dream," then that's fine. I trust You.*

God *(burying His face in His hands as I hyperventilate into a bag)*: *Oh Elizabeth, where do I even start with you?*

How do you respond when life changes unexpectedly? What excites you? What scares you? What kinds of conversations do you have with God?

....

....

....

....

....

....

....

The angel went to [Mary] and said, "Greetings, you who are highly favored! The Lord is with you." Mary was greatly troubled at his words and wondered what kind of greeting this might be. But the angel said to her, "Do not be afraid, Mary; you have found favor with God. You will conceive and give birth to a son, and you are to call him Jesus." . . ."How will this be," Mary asked the angel, "since I am a virgin?" The angel answered, "The Holy Spirit will come on you, and the power of the Most High will overshadow you. So the holy one to be born will be called the Son of God."
LUKE 1:28–31, 34–35

Sometimes God says, "Go," and then points us to a place we never imagined. Never wanted. When Gabriel told Mary she was to bear God's Son, she didn't just silently accept the news—she asked a respectful question to clarify her expectations and her role: "How will this be, since I am a virgin?" Considering the fertility technology of the day, it was a valid question!

But think about all the questions Mary could have asked Gabriel:

"Why me?"

"Can you talk me through exactly who this boy is going to be when He grows up?"

"Are you sure I won't be stoned for this? And can I get that guaranteed in writing?"

But faithful Mary asks none of those questions. She doesn't ask for favors or assurances of safety and happiness—she just asks for greater understanding. And Gabriel is happy to give it.

What feelings, fears, and faith questions do you face when life changes unexpectedly?

....

....

....

....

....

....

....

....

....

"I am the Lord's servant," Mary answered.
"May your word to me be fulfilled." Then the angel left her.

LUKE 1:38

Mary's example shows us that it's okay to ask God, "Hey, Father, how is this going to go? I see where You are pointing me—now how do I get there?"

When God hands us change, it is not necessarily sinful to ask why, nor is it wrong to take the time we need to process the change (see the Psalms for examples of prayers like this).

Mary's example points us to the place of faith where we eventually want to arrive. She simply says, "I am the Lord's servant. May it be to me as you have said."

What inspires you about Mary's attitude? What challenges you?

....

....

....

....

....

....

....

....

....

....

....

"My Father, if it is not possible for this cup to be taken away unless I drink it, may your will be done."

MATTHEW 26:42

How much energy and time—how much life—do we waste fighting change that has already happened? The die is cast, the deed is done, but like stubborn children we throw ourselves on the floor, kicking and wailing, "It's not fair! I didn't ask for this! My life might have been so different!" Fair or not, the change has happened. And we can't go forward if we're pouting in a corner or throwing tantrums on the floor. (*Ahem.* I may or may not have done this. I may or may not have done this a lot of times. And like Forrest Gump, "That's all I have to say about that.")

What new fears are you facing today that you didn't face in your younger years? In what new areas of life do you need courage?

Whoever watches the wind will not plant;
whoever looks at the clouds will not reap.

Ecclesiastes 11:4

Practically speaking, "what might have been" is a waste of time. A waste of life. Because what might have been can never be—it is fantasy. If we sit around wind-watching—dreaming about the "good old days," wishing our lives away—we will never plant seeds in our new lives; if we never plant seeds, we can never reap joy.

Picture yourself happy and fulfilled in life—not in the future, but in the situation you are living in right now. What seeds do you need to plant to help that joy and fulfillment come about? Do you need to let go of a disappointment? Embrace a particular role? Invest in new relationships? Learn to love a new place or people? Journal your thoughts.

....

....

....

....

....

....

....

....

....

....

....

....

Yet to all who did receive him, to those who believed in his name,
he gave the right to become children of God—children born
not of natural descent, nor of human decision
or a husband's will, but born of God.
JOHN 1:12–13

Let us choose to open our hearts to new situations. Find home in new places. Give our hearts to new people. When circumstances change, let us give God a chance to reveal His goodness, His wisdom, and His faithfulness no matter where we go.

When has God seen you through an unanticipated change? How specifically did He provide for your needs (physical, spiritual, emotional, relational)?

....

....

....

....

....

....

....

....

....

....

....

....

....

"My soul glorifies the Lord and my spirit rejoices in God my Savior, for he has been mindful of the humble state of his servant. From now on all generations will call me blessed, for the Mighty One has done great things for me—holy is his name."
LUKE 1:46-49

We may not get to choose when or how life changes, but we do get to choose how we respond. When God brings change, let us find the faith to say, "I am the Lord's servant."

Ready for a creative spiritual exercise? Try this: In the space provided, write a letter to last-year you something like. . .You don't know this yet, but soon you are going to go through (fill in the blank). You are going to respond by (fill in the blank). You will wish you could see where you are after one year, because even though it's difficult, God comforts you and takes care of you by (fill in the blank).

....

....

....

....

....

....

....

....

....

....

....

....

I will instruct you and teach you in the way you should go;
I will counsel you with my loving eye on you.

PSALM 32:8

When questions go unanswered and our future looks cloudy, let us remain confident in God's kindness.

On this page, begin assembling a list of scriptures that help you to find courage or feel safe in God's care. Add to the list over time, reading through the verses often.

....

....

....

....

....

....

....

....

....

....

....

....

....

....

....

....

"But the Advocate, the Holy Spirit, whom the Father will send in my name, will teach you all things and will remind you of everything I have said to you."

John 14:26

....

....

....

....

....

....

....

....

....

....

....

....

....

....

....

....

Have you ever noticed how many times in the Bible God calls His people to remember? *Reminds* us to remember? He even builds remembrance into our lives and our worship. When it's time to find courage for a new stage of life, or time to find a whole new kind of courage, let's start moving forward by looking backward. Finding faith for the future by borrowing from the past. I don't mean looking back and saying, "Wow, I wish I could go back to the good old days"—no. Let's look back and remember times when we've been brave before, and it was worth it. Times when life was difficult but God saw us through.

Write down a description of one of the scariest or most painful seasons in your life. Now, write down the specific ways God protected you, comforted you, rescued you, or gave you the strength and encouragement to make it through that time. Be as detailed as you can—did He provide money? Energy? Grace instead of punishment? Just the right friend at just the right time? Prepare to stand amazed at the kindness and provision of God. Spend some time in prayer thanking Him for His care.

....

....

....

....

....

....

....

....

....

Jesus replied, "The hour has come for the Son of Man to be glorified. Very truly I tell you, unless a kernel of wheat falls to the ground and dies, it remains only a single seed. But if it dies, it produces many seeds. Anyone who loves their life will lose it, while anyone who hates their life in this world will keep it for eternal life. Whoever serves me must follow me; and where I am, my servant also will be. My Father will honor the one who serves me. Now my soul is troubled, and what shall I say? 'Father, save me from this hour'? No, it was for this very reason I came to this hour. Father, glorify your name!"

JOHN 12:23-28

Jesus was born so that He might serve for a time but then suffer and die. Just because something is difficult, controversial, or painful doesn't mean it is outside the will of God. Few of us would choose suffering for ourselves, but God's big-picture plan sometimes involves injustice and pain. His path for us is often more difficult than the one we would choose for ourselves.

Write about a time when you have seen God bring great good out of great suffering.

....

....

....

....

....

....

....

....

....

....

....

....

"You are the light of the world. A town built on a hill cannot be hidden. Neither do people light a lamp and put it under a bowl. Instead they put it on its stand, and it gives light to everyone in the house."
MATTHEW 5:14–15

Sometimes God tells us to go *and stay*:
Stay home.
Go back to an old place with a new attitude.
Show His grace to our family.
Share His love with our neighbors.
Go deep.
Love hard.
Grow strong.

▶

What are some other ways that God could be telling you to "go and stay"?

....

....

....

....

....

....

....

....

....

....

....

....

"Though the mountains be shaken and the hills be removed, yet my unfailing love for you will not be shaken nor my covenant of peace be removed," says the Lord, who has compassion on you.

Isaiah 54:10

Being righteous doesn't mean we don't face troubles. In fact, we may face *many*. But no trouble is bigger than our God, no failure is beyond redemption, and great heartache draws Him near.

We think of mountains as permanent things, huge and unshakable. But sometimes even mountains fall. And when mountains in our lives are shaken—marriage, family, health, everything that makes us who we are—God's love remains. When all else changes, when it seems the whole world is falling apart, God's love never changes. God's love never fails.

List some scriptures that remind you that God's love never changes, never fails. (Need some starting points? Try Isaiah 46:3–4; 49:15–16; 63:9; Deuteronomy 1:29–31; Zephaniah 3:17.) Read them until you believe them. (This might take a while—you might want to read them daily.)

*The eyes of the L*ORD *are on the righteous, and his ears are attentive to their cry. . . . The righteous cry out, and the L*ORD *hears them; he delivers them from all their troubles. The L*ORD *is close to the brokenhearted and saves those who are crushed in spirit. The righteous person may have many troubles, but the L*ORD *delivers him from them all.*
PSALM 34:15, 17–19

None of us plan to suffer. None of us plan to grieve. To fail at something we longed to achieve. To remain single forever and ever. To become single again after marriage. To face infertility. To battle chronic illness, endless pain. To feel crippled by anxiety or depression. To watch a beloved child go astray. To lose people we love before their time. Losses like these often happen out of our control and out of the blue. One day life is dandy, we're happy and free, and then—*wham*—life turns on us. (And if we're honest, in the dark, secret corners of our hearts, we may even feel that *God Himself* has turned on us.)

Have you ever felt like God turned His back on you? Journal how you felt, and why. How did you find your way back to Him?

....

....

....

....

....

....

....

....

....

....

Satisfy us in the morning with your unfailing love, that we may sing for joy and be glad all our days. Make us glad for as many days as you have afflicted us, for as many years as we have seen trouble. May your deeds be shown to your servants, your splendor to their children.

PSALM 90:14–16

There is great courage in facing grief. In starting over. In learning to live again, to love again, after great loss.

How has God helped you or someone you love to start over after heartache?

....

....

....

....

....

....

....

....

....

....

....

....

....

....

....

Many are the plans in a person's heart,
but it is the LORD's purpose that prevails.

PROVERBS 19:21

It takes true humility and total surrender to give control to God. To say, "You know better than I do." Or, in the words of Jesus: "Yet not as I will, but as You will."

How do you feel when you finally surrender to God?

....

....

....

....

....

....

....

....

....

....

....

....

....

....

....

....

"Are not five sparrows sold for two pennies? Yet not one of them is forgotten by God. Indeed, the very hairs of your head are all numbered. Don't be afraid; you are worth more than many sparrows."

LUKE 12:6–7

Sometimes problems arise and we manage to find a way around them. We just change direction and—*woo-hoo!*—we've sidestepped the crisis. When that happens, yay for us. But sometimes God has us in circumstances we can't escape. No way around, no way out. Sometimes He puts us in, or allows us to remain in, situations that expose our every doubt, fear, and weakness. They range from the inconvenient to the catastrophic: A class you can't drop. A conflict you can't avoid. A financial disaster. A family drama. A sick child. An unexpected death.

Have you ever felt stuck in a hard situation? Faced a time when you asked God to rescue you and it seemed like He had other plans? What was the final outcome, and what did you learn from it?

....

....

....

....

....

....

....

....

....

....

....

....

*Yet, my brothers, I do not consider myself to have "arrived,"
spiritually, nor do I consider myself already perfect. But I keep
going on, grasping ever more firmly that purpose for which Christ
grasped me. My brothers, I do not consider myself to have fully
grasped it even now. But I do concentrate on this: I leave the past
behind and with hands outstretched to whatever lies ahead
I go straight for the goal—my reward the honour
of being called by God in Christ.*
PHILIPPIANS 3:12-14 PHILLIPS

Christians are no better than anyone else, but thanks to the grace of God, the blood of Christ, and the power of the Spirit, you and I get to grow and change. What a wondrous, liberating gift! You know all those flaws you hate about yourself? Those weaknesses that frustrate you, embarrass you, and limit you? With God's help we can change them! We can grow. *We can grow*, and what a privilege that is!

Write about some of the growth you have already experienced as a Christian. How are you different from the person you used to be? How have you already made God proud?

....

....

....

....

....

....

....

....

....

....

....

....

....

Yet I am always with you; you hold me by my right hand. You guide me with your counsel, and afterward you will take me into glory.
PSALM 73:23-24

The thing is, with God on our side, very few things are actually *can't*-level things.

And can we be honest about what we're really saying when we say, "I can't"? When we say, "I can't," most of the time we're really saying, "I won't."

Write about a time when you told God, "I can't." What was really standing in the way of your "yes" to Him?

....

....

....

....

....

....

....

....

....

....

....

....

....

But we have this treasure in jars of clay to show that this all-surpassing power is from God and not from us. We are hard pressed on every side, but not crushed; perplexed, but not in despair; persecuted, but not abandoned; struck down, but not destroyed. We always carry around in our body the death of Jesus, so that the life of Jesus may also be revealed in our body. For we who are alive are always being given over to death for Jesus' sake, so that his life may also be revealed in our mortal body.
2 Corinthians 4:7–11

When we say, "I can't," we write off God's power, His promises. And what is the alternative anyway? The next time you are tempted to shut down, to run off, to stop growing; the next time you are tempted to shout, "But Lord, I can't," remember this: Maybe *you* can't. . .but God can. And maybe, with God, you already are.

Has God ever proven you wrong when you told Him, "I can't"? How?

....

....

....

....

....

....

....

....

....

....

....

....

....

....

He guides the humble in what is right and teaches them his way.
All the ways of the LORD are loving and faithful toward
those who keep the demands of his covenant.
PSALM 25:9-10

Feelings are beautiful, a wondrous gift from God—the ability to be happy so hard it hurts, to laugh, to rant, to mourn, to love. But as with all of God's gifts, Satan wants to flip those blessings around and warp them for his purposes.

To turn our capacity for love into selfish obsession.

To turn our admiration of beautiful things into greed.

To turn innocent friendship into inappropriate attraction.

To turn godly sorrow into crippling regret.

To turn our desire for peace into addictive behavior.

To turn healthy grief into destructive depression.

Write a prayer to God, asking Him to help you manage your feelings. Ask Him to help you know when you can trust your feelings and when you should listen to Him instead.

....

....

....

....

....

....

....

....

....

....

....

*Dear children, let's not merely say that we love each other;
let us show the truth by our actions. Our actions will show that
we belong to the truth, so we will be confident when we stand
before God. Even if we feel guilty, God is greater than our
feelings, and he knows everything. Dear friends, if we don't
feel guilty, we can come to God with bold confidence.*

1 JOHN 3:18–21 NLT

Feelings are complicated, but God's wise guidelines in the scriptures can help give our emotions healthy, godly boundaries.

Which emotions do you find most difficult to manage? What scriptures help you direct those feelings?

....

....

....

....

....

....

....

....

....

....

....

....

....

....

*"I have told you all this so that you may have peace in me.
Here on earth you will have many trials and sorrows.
But take heart, because I have overcome the world."*

John 16:33 NLT

....

....

....

....

....

....

....

....

....

....

....

....

....

....

....

....

....

....

Any among us who have endured chronic emotional suffering—depression, anxiety, addiction, mental illness, eating disorders, self-harm—may find great comfort in scripture. Although we are not promised "easy fixes" for our afflictions, we are offered guidance and hope. Hope that there are no powers Christ cannot overcome, no chains He cannot break. And that His power is made perfect in our weakness.

How has God already helped you to grow in your emotional well-being, and how would you like Him to help you continue to grow?

....

....

....

....

....

....

....

....

....

....

....

....

....

....

I urge you to live a life worthy of the calling you have received.

EPHESIANS 4:1

s there something you have refused to change—or been afraid to change—until now? Some pet sin, some limiting weakness? Take a look around at the people you love and ask yourself if your inaction is affecting others.

Are your current fears and choices affecting someone else? What might you need to change to have a positive impact?

....

....

....

....

....

....

....

....

....

....

....

....

....

....

As for me, may I never boast about anything except the cross of our Lord Jesus Christ. Because of that cross, my interest in this world has been crucified, and the world's interest in me has also died.

GALATIANS 6:14 NLT

In the end, *love* is why we change. When we want to stay the same, love forces our hand. When it's easier to hide in a hole, to stay safe on the ground, we change because we love.

Can you identify a weakness in your life that can't stay the same? What first step would help you to begin changing it?

....

....

....

....

....

....

....

....

....

....

....

....

....

....

....

....

For those who are led by the Spirit of God are the children of God. The Spirit you received does not make you slaves, so that you live in fear again; rather, the Spirit you received brought about your adoption to sonship. And by him we cry, "Abba, Father." The Spirit himself testifies with our spirit that we are God's children. Now if we are children, then we are heirs—heirs of God and co-heirs with Christ, if indeed we share in his sufferings in order that we may also share in his glory. I consider that our present sufferings are not worth comparing with the glory that will be revealed in us.

ROMANS 8:14–18

Has *life* happened to you? Joys so staggering you can't put them into words, can't share them with anyone but God? Gifts so precious and rare that their worth consumes you, overwhelms you—makes you vulnerable, your heart no longer your own—and you know if you lose the gift you'll shatter beyond repair?

Has life thrown you detours and delays you never expected? Hurts and betrayals you want to forgive but cannot forget? Disappointments and regrets that haunt your thoughts and steal your contentment? We all live life and we all have scars.

Spend time this week praying through your life, thanking God for blessings and miracles He has already given. Thank Him for providing in times of need. Thank Him for times when He has stood beside you in your grief, comforting you and letting you cry. Thank Him for seeing you through this season of your life with all its challenges. And thank Him in faith for blessings and miracles yet to come. Begin writing your prayer here.

....

....

....

....

....

....

....

....

....

God is our refuge and strength, an ever-present help in trouble.
Therefore we will not fear, though the earth give way and the
mountains fall into the heart of the sea, though its waters
roar and foam and the mountains quake with their surging.
PSALM 46:1-3

Have you been brave for God in the past? Have you gone all in before, but somewhere along the way you took a step back? Have you pulled back your heart—forgotten your role, lost your way? Stepped in to pull God aside, to whisper in His ear, "Hey, this isn't the plan—this isn't what You promised me. Let's go back home"?

Take a minute to ask yourself, What would it look like if I gave Jesus everything again? What would it look like if I was brave again at this stage of my life? Journal your thoughts below.

....

....

....

....

....

....

....

....

....

....

....

....

....

"Listen to me, you descendants of Jacob, all the remnant of the people of Israel, you whom I have upheld since your birth, and have carried since you were born. Even to your old age and gray hairs I am he, I am he who will sustain you. I have made you and I will carry you; I will sustain you and I will rescue you."
ISAIAH 46:3-4

Finding courage isn't just a young person's game. It's not something you master once and never face again. No, finding courage is a lifelong pursuit. The older we get, the more vulnerable and weak we may feel. The older we get, the more we have to risk; the older we get, the more we have to lose.

As you grow older, do you find it more difficult to be brave, or is courage coming more easily? Why?

....

....

....

....

....

....

....

....

....

....

....

....

....

"For I am the LORD your God who takes hold of your right hand and says to you, Do not fear; I will help you."

ISAIAH 41:13

The fear "disorders":

- Too Good to Be True Syndrome
- Hyperactive Self-Criticism Condition
- God Made a Mistake Disorder
- Just Kidding I Didn't Mean to Pray That Prayer Disease (because now God said yes and I have to be brave)
- That's Too Scary So I Won't Even Try It Disorder (which is closely related to. . .)
- That's Too Hard So Let's Pretend God Didn't Say It Disorder
- If I Don't Try I Can't Fail Syndrome
- I've Been Hurt Before So I'd Rather Stay Safe Disease

Which of the "fear disorders" do you struggle with? List some scriptures that can help you to combat them.

....

....

....

....

....

....

....

....

....

....

....

When I am afraid, I put my trust in you.

PSALM 56:3

Sometimes the greatest courage is in strapping on skis with trembling hands, V-plowing down the mountain all the way to the bottom.

Sometimes the greatest courage is in flailing around the kitchen, tears streaming down, but then sitting back down at the table. Picking up the pen and filling in one blank, then another, then another.

Sometimes the greatest courage is in getting up after a fall, showing our face again to people who have seen us fail.

Jot down a description of the scariest times in your life and how you felt God's presence. In what specific ways did He protect you, comfort you, rescue you, or give you the strength and encouragement to make it through?

....

....

....

....

....

....

....

....

....

....

....

....

*Be my rock of refuge, to which I can always go. . . . For you have
been my hope, Sovereign Lord, my confidence since my youth.
From birth I have relied on you; you brought me forth
from my mother's womb. I will ever praise you.*
PSALM 71:3, 5-6

Sometimes the greatest courage is in sloughing off shame and regret—heavy weights, crippling chains—to stand tall in God's grace and say, "Here I am, Lord. Here I am to fight another day." Trusting that the God who holds the earth in His hands also holds *us* near His heart.

How have shame or regret hindered you from answering God's call? What would change if you found the courage to accept God's grace?

This is what the LORD says—your Redeemer, the Holy One of Israel:
"I am the LORD your God, who teaches you what is best
for you, who directs you in the way you should go."

ISAIAH 48:17

God's word casts light on the potholes and boundary lines. Although scripture may not give us an exact answer—*Should I seek a new job? Should I get a master's degree?*—it can often provide us with healthy parameters.

What intimidates you most about making big decisions? Have you ever felt insecure or paralyzed? Why?

The Lord foils the plans of the nations; he thwarts the purposes of the peoples. But the plans of the Lord stand firm forever, the purposes of his heart through all generations.
Psalm 33:10-11

When can we be confident that God *is* calling a person? The scriptures are filled with universal calls (you could also call them commands or expectations) that apply to all believers, and we can share those calls with one other with confidence. All Christians are called to love God with all our heart, soul, mind, and strength; to love our neighbor as ourselves; to serve the poor; to be devoted members of the body of Christ; and the list goes on. When in doubt, let us speak with humility and with words that reflect scripture.

Compile a list of scriptures that can help you—and people you love—in making wise decisions.

....

....

....

....

....

....

....

....

....

....

....

....

*The LORD makes firm the steps of the one who delights in him;
though he may stumble, he will not fall, for the
LORD upholds him with his hand.*
PSALM 37:23–24

In many of life's decisions, we don't get specific instructions. We get options. Which means something amazing. . .and empowering: *God trusts us to make a decision for ourselves.* His only rule? That we enjoy our free choice within His loving limits.

What steps do you typically follow when making big life decisions? How do you ensure your choices fall within God's boundaries?

....

....

....

....

....

....

....

....

....

....

....

....

....

....

· ·

"The LORD will guide you always; he will satisfy your needs in a sun-scorched land and will strengthen your frame. You will be like a well-watered garden, like a spring whose waters never fail."

ISAIAH 58:11

· ·

God has entrusted humans, His last and greatest masterpiece, with the gift, the honor, the privilege, of decision-making. He has created us to depend on Him for life and breath, for salvation and wisdom, but He has also given us freedom to choose our own path and to *align* that path with His ways and His will.

Which means. . .

We get to choose what to do after high school.

We get to choose to stay single, or if we want to marry, we get to choose a spouse. (Of course, they have to choose us too—that's the maddening part.)

We get to choose a career.

We get to choose a city to live in and a specific apartment or house to live in.

We get to choose if and when we try to get pregnant or adopt a child.

What choices are you currently considering in life? Write a prayer here thanking God for His trust in you and asking Him for wisdom and guidance.

....

....

....

....

....

....

....

....

Your word is a lamp for my feet, a light on my path.

PSALM 119:105

Scripture illuminates our path. When we shine biblical principles on our decisions, our path is made clearer. Scripture gives us boundaries and limits our choices (in a good way). When we do our best to live according to biblical principles, we can be sure that God is pleased with us and that we have His blessing no matter what we decide.

In what ways can boundaries and limits be good? What scriptures have guided you the most in life? How might they help you as you weigh your current choices?

....

....

....

....

....

....

....

....

....

....

....

....

Plans fail when there is no counsel,
but with many advisers they succeed.
PROVERBS 15:22 HCSB

The Bible is clear: godly advice is a good thing! Seek counsel from spiritual people who know God's Word and know you. They can help you sort through the options and feelings, keeping God and His principles in mind.

Whose life, faith, and decision-making do you admire? How can you invite godly counsel into your life?

....

....

....

....

....

....

....

....

....

....

....

....

....

....

....

For this God is our God for ever and ever;
he will be our guide even to the end.

Psalm 48:14

It is difficult to hear the voice of God when our ears, our minds, and our hearts are constantly pulled in five million directions by phones, by posts, and even by people. If you think you are being called to go somewhere or do something new for God, before you move ahead, take some time. Time to calm your spirit and still your mind. Time to examine your heart—your motives, your gifts, your needs. Time to lie still as Samuel did and pray, "Speak, Lord, for Your servant is listening."

Stop and listen to God today. Read His Word and meditate on its truths. If you have fears and concerns about a decision you need to make, describe them here and pray about them.

Teach me to do your will, for you are my God;
may your good Spirit lead me on level ground.
PSALM 143:10

We need to listen to God, but we also need to speak with Him. When we are making a big decision, it is both wise and biblical to set aside special time for prayer. We see this example numerous times in scripture: Before beginning His ministry, Jesus spent forty days alone with God. Before selecting His twelve disciples, Jesus spent a night alone in prayer. Before going to the cross, Jesus prepared Himself in the Garden of Gethsemane.

What decision do you most need guidance for right now? What would a special prayer time look like as you weigh your decision?

....

....

....

....

....

....

....

....

....

....

....

....

Guide me in your truth and teach me, for you are God my Savior, and my hope is in you all day long.

PSALM 25:5

Feelings are *a* factor in our decision-making, but not the *only* factor. Feelings are fickle. Feelings can be affected by everything from hormones, to caffeine, to lack of caffeine, to medications, to conflict, to Facebook feeds, to Kleenex commercials, to thoughtless comments from friends, to last night's dinner, to—no, I'm not kidding—the stage of the moon and the presence of cats. Feelings are an unreliable—even dangerous—way to gauge truth or determine the will of God.

What role do feelings play in your decision-making? How is making a decision based on a "gut feeling" different than basing your decisions on scripture, prayer, and godly counsel? Try this: pair up with a friend to share a decision in which you need God's guidance, and pray for each other every day this week.

....

....

....

....

....

....

....

....

....

....

....

May he work in us what is pleasing to him, through Jesus Christ,
to whom be glory for ever and ever. Amen.
HEBREWS 13:21

When a decision brings difficulty or heartache into our lives, does that mean we have made a bad choice? Maybe. Maybe not. Sometimes life is just hard no matter what we do. No matter what we choose. Sometimes we find ourselves caught between the proverbial rock and hard place, and the best outcome we can hope for is "not horrible" (aka "not being squished").

We see this concept at work in the lives of our biblical ancestors: obedience and sacrifice for God often brought difficulty, pain, and loss into their lives. But no one would suggest that their obedience was a wrong decision! Let us be careful not to misinterpret misfortune as a sign of God's disapproval.

Have you ever doubted your decisions when things didn't turn out the way you had hoped? What did you learn from that difficulty?

....

....

....

....

....

....

....

....

....

....

Look to the LORD and his strength; seek his face always.
1 CHRONICLES 16:11

We do not serve a vague God. If God has a strong opinion about what you need to do in a certain situation, He is powerful enough to find a way to speak *clearly*—through scripture, through advisers, or by opening or shutting a door.

Has God ever slammed a door in your life? In what ways did He make it clear it wasn't the right opportunity for you?

....

....

....

....

....

....

....

....

....

....

....

....

....

....

As you endure this divine discipline, remember that God is treating you as his own children. Who ever heard of a child who is never disciplined by its father? If God doesn't discipline you as he does all of his children, it means that you are illegitimate and are not really his children at all. Since we respected our earthly fathers who disciplined us, shouldn't we submit even more to the discipline of the Father of our spirits, and live forever? For our earthly fathers disciplined us for a few years, doing the best they knew how. But God's discipline is always good for us, so that we might share in his holiness. No discipline is enjoyable while it is happening—it's painful! But afterward there will be a peaceful harvest of right living for those who are trained in this way.

HEBREWS 12:7-11 NLT

So what if you *do* make a not-so-great choice? God doesn't abandon us just because we make imperfect decisions. Just as a good parent loves and supports and encourages a child through a difficult season in life—even if that season is self-inflicted and ill advised—so God does not leave us alone, even when we make a less-than-best choice.

Have you ever made a less-than-perfect decision but seen God make lemonade out of your lemons? Write about that time.

• •

I could go on and on, but I've run out of time. There are so many more—Gideon, Barak, Samson, Jephthah, David, Samuel, the prophets. . . . Through acts of faith, they toppled kingdoms, made justice work, took the promises for themselves. . . . Not one of these people, even though their lives of faith were exemplary, got their hands on what was promised. God had a better plan for us: that their faith and our faith would come together to make one completed whole, their lives of faith not complete apart from ours.

HEBREWS 11:32–33, 39–40 MSG

• •

....

....

....

....

....

....

....

....

....

....

....

....

Sometimes the path of righteousness leads us not to quiet waters but "through the valley of the shadow of death" (Psalm 23:4 KJV). We are not promised escape from the shadows, but enough light to find our footing. We are not promised freedom from trouble, but strength to survive whatever trouble comes.

Think about a righteous Bible character who obeyed God but experienced hardship because of, or in the midst of, their obedience. How does their story encourage you?

And so, dear brothers and sisters, I plead with you to give your bodies to God because of all he has done for you. Let them be a living and holy sacrifice—the kind he will find acceptable. This is truly the way to worship him.

ROMANS 12:1 NLT

We honor God—we bring Him glory and praise, we celebrate His marvelous creation and honor His endless creativity—when we use the gifts He has given us. Giving ourselves to God—our bodies, our personalities, our strengths, our energies, our hearts, our talents—is an act of worship.

How do you feel when you offer your gifts to God? Do you have a gift you have hesitated to use for Him? Why?

....

....

....

....

....

....

....

....

....

....

....

....

....

We have different gifts, according to the grace given to each of us. If your gift is prophesying, then prophesy in accordance with your faith; if it is serving, then serve; if it is teaching, then teach; if it is to encourage, then give encouragement; if it is giving, then give generously; if it is to lead, do it diligently; if it is to show mercy, do it cheerfully.

ROMANS 12:6-8

*I*n His grace God has gifted us all. Our gifts are His grace. No gift is more valuable than another; they—and we—are all needed to build up God's church. If one gift is missing, the entire body of Christ suffers loss.

Have fun brainstorming one new way in which you might use one of your gifts for God. Can you serve in some new way at church or in your community? Can you serve a neighbor or meet a friend's need? (If your idea doesn't sound fun or inspire you in some way, chances are, it's not the right fit. If you get stuck, ask a friend to help you brainstorm.)

"Watch out! Don't do your good deeds publicly, to be admired by others, for you will lose the reward from your Father in heaven. When you give to someone in need, don't do as the hypocrites do—blowing trumpets in the synagogues and streets to call attention to their acts of charity! I tell you the truth, they have received all the reward they will ever get. But when you give to someone in need, don't let your left hand know what your right hand is doing. Give your gifts in private, and your Father, who sees everything, will reward you." . . . So let's not get tired of doing what is good. At just the right time we will reap a harvest of blessing if we don't give up.

MATTHEW 6:1-4; GALATIANS 6:9 NLT

Serving God isn't always loud and dramatic and full of transition; most of the time it's quiet. It's humble. It's simple. And it's hard work.

When you picture yourself doing valuable work for God, what comes to mind? How does it change your perspective to remember that small acts of quiet service mean a lot to God?

....

....

....

....

....

....

....

....

....

....

....

....

....

....

....

Do nothing out of selfish ambition or vain conceit. Rather, in humility value others above yourselves, not looking to your own interests but each of you to the interests of the others. In your relationships with one another, have the same mindset as Christ Jesus: Who, being in very nature God, did not consider equality with God something to be used to his own advantage; rather, he made himself nothing by taking the very nature of a servant, being made in human likeness. And being found in appearance as a man, he humbled himself by becoming obedient to death—even death on a cross!

PHILIPPIANS 2:3-8

Have you ever felt like your gifts aren't as shiny as other people's? Like your contributions to your family, your workplace, your friends, or God's church all seem so. . .small? As Zechariah 4:10 says, "Who dares despise the day of small things?" God sees small things. He values them. As Jesus celebrated the two coins donated by the poor widow—all she had to live on—so God honors the humblest responses to His lofty call (Mark 12:41–43).

How do you feel about the gifts God has given you? How do you think God feels about the gifts He gave you? What does He feel when He watches you use them?

Fan into flame the gift of God.
2 Timothy 1:6

Don't dismiss or undervalue your gifts just because they come easily. Use them! Expand them! Enjoy them! Offer them to God to use as He wills.

How can you further develop your God-given gifts and talents? Make a list of ideas and goals here.

....

....

....

....

....

....

....

....

....

....

....

....

....

....

The human body has many parts, but the many parts make up one whole body. So it is with the body of Christ.

1 CORINTHIANS 12:12 NLT

We tend to picture a call from almighty God as some grandiose, glorious exploit—slaying a giant, saving the day—and sometimes it is. But sometimes God calls us to do quiet things. "Small" things. Step-aside things.

Have you ever served God by stepping aside or serving behind the scenes? How did it feel? How was that kind of service rewarding in a different way from the times when you have been recognized for your sacrifice?

....

....

....

....

....

....

....

....

....

....

....

....

....

A generous person will prosper;
whoever refreshes others will be refreshed.
PROVERBS 11:25

How do we identify our spiritual gifts? Here are a few diagnostic questions to ask yourself:

- What do you like to do?
- What do you naturally do well? What comes easily to you? (If you're not sure, ask your family and friends.)
- What are other people always asking you to do for them?
- What do you gravitate toward doing in your spare time?
- What do you often get compliments for doing?
- What would you do in the church—how would you serve—if you didn't care what people thought?

Answer the diagnostic questions in the space provided. What are your gifts, and how might God want you to use them for His church?

....

....

....

....

....

....

....

....

....

....

....

....

Better is one day in your courts than a thousand elsewhere;
I would rather be a doorkeeper in the house of my God
than dwell in the tents of the wicked.

PSALM 84:10

Your role may not be glamorous, it may not be up front, it may be quiet and behind the scenes, but if you use your gifts to serve God, then you are fulfilling your calling. Your heart will be full and your Father will be proud.

In what ways do you think you make God proud?

....

....

....

....

....

....

....

....

....

....

....

....

....

....

....

Whatever you do, work at it with all your heart,
as working for the Lord, not for human masters.
COLOSSIANS 3:23

Jesus calls us to serve where we are, with what we already have, and with our whole heart—even if we aren't crazy about our current situation or responsibility. When we do, perhaps one day we will be entrusted with more (see Matthew 25:14-30).

Think about the ways you are currently serving God or His people. Are you frustrated or discontent with your role in any way? If so, how can you address those feelings?

I have been crucified with Christ and I no longer live, but Christ lives in me. The life I now live in the body, I live by faith in the Son of God, who loved me and gave himself for me.

GALATIANS 2:20

When we study the lives of men and women called by God in scripture, we see that their callings usually brought more difficulty than celebrity. More pain than fame. I say that not to discourage us from answering God's call, but to help us adjust our expectations and motivations. To encourage us when our gifts, our role, and our call are different than others'—or different than what we may have envisioned for ourselves. Answering God's call means embracing the way of Jesus: the way of humility, sacrifice, and service. Giving up yourself, your place, your rights.

When you picture doing something great for God, what comes to mind? In what ways might you need to redefine spiritual greatness?

....

....

....

....

....

....

....

....

....

....

....

....

As Jesus was getting into the boat, the man who had been demon-possessed begged to go with him. Jesus did not let him, but said, "Go home to your own people and tell them how much the Lord has done for you, and how he has had mercy on you." So the man went away and began to tell in the Decapolis how much Jesus had done for him. And all the people were amazed.

Mark 5:18-20

Right now God may not be calling you to move to a new city or seek a new job or assume a new role. God always wants us to move forward, but that forward motion often happens right where we are, in the life we already have, among people we already know.

How do you know if God is telling you to go or to go and stay?

....

....

....

....

....

....

....

....

....

....

....

....

....

....

Do not conform to the pattern of this world, but be transformed by the renewing of your mind. Then you will be able to test and approve what God's will is—his good, pleasing and perfect will.

ROMANS 12:2

A new city won't automatically change us. A job change won't change us. A new relationship won't change us. Change happens in only one place, a place we carry with us everywhere: change happens in our hearts.

In what ways do you rely on external changes to pave the way for spiritual change? How can you change even if your circumstances remain the same?

....

....

....

....

....

....

....

....

....

....

....

....

....

....

"As for me and my household, we will serve the Lord."

Joshua 24:15

No matter where we live or what our role may be, we can change, we can grow, and we can bravely give ourselves to God.

What best describes your emotional response to difficulty? . . .a puddle of tears, shutting down and shutting up, pretending nothing is wrong, complaining to friends, resenting the difficulty, looking for someone to blame?

Now describe how you would like to respond to difficulty, and begin praying that God will help you to respond in a new way. You won't change overnight, but with God's help you can grow emotionally stronger!

....

....

....

....

....

....

....

....

....

....

....

....

We know what real love is because Jesus gave up his life for us. So we also ought to give up our lives for our brothers and sisters. If someone has enough money to live well and sees a brother or sister in need but shows no compassion—how can God's love be in that person? Dear children, let's not merely say that we love each other; let us show the truth by our actions.
1 JOHN 3:16–18 NLT

How many times do we unintentionally overlook opportunities for serving Christ in our daily lives? We miss them because we see them all the time. Our eyes—and hearts—skip past familiar needs, old heartaches, because familiarity has bred blindness. Dullness. Life gets busy, our schedule gets tight, and we accidentally walk past lonely neighbors needing friends. Classmates struggling with depression. Recent divorcées longing for a listening ear. New parents needing a hot meal or a kind word. Colossians 4 urges us, "Devote yourselves to prayer, being watchful and thankful. . . . Be wise in the way you act toward outsiders; make the most of every opportunity" (verses 2, 5). Jesus often lamented dullness, saying, "Do you have eyes but fail to see, and ears but fail to hear?" (Mark 8:18). Let us pray to see and hear the needs around us.

Jesus said, "The harvest is plentiful but the workers are few" (Matthew 9:37). Try this: Every day this week, pray to have the eyes of Christ as you look around your school, your neighborhood, your workplace. Before you leave the house every morning, ask God to show you needs He would like you to meet. Write your first prayer here.

....

....

....

....

....

....

....

....

Day after day, in the temple courts and from house to house, they never stopped teaching and proclaiming the good news that Jesus is the Messiah.

ACTS 5:42

have always loved this little phrase hiding in the book of Acts: "from house to house." Yes, the apostles shared Christ in the temple, but they also went from house to house. Sometimes the most important ministry takes place quietly—at kitchen tables and on back porches, in living rooms and in backyards.

How might you imitate the apostles' example in your daily life?

*Never be lacking in zeal, but keep your
spiritual fervor, serving the Lord.*

ROMANS 12:11

Have you been feeling bored and uninspired, twiddling your thumbs and waiting for God to say, "Go"? Waiting for Him to call you to something new and exciting? *I want to go for it for God, but first He needs to change my circumstances. . . .* But consider this: Maybe God has *already* said, "Go!" Maybe He said, "Go," long ago when He put you in your current situation—but you got there and never really *went.* Your body arrived, but your heart stayed somewhere else. As soon as you got there, you sat down on the job. Pulled up an armchair and put up your feet. Got comfortable. A bit complacent. You may be itching to go somewhere else, but what if God already has you exactly where He wants you during this time in your life? Perhaps God's message to you is, "Stay put but *get going*!" Sometimes it's not our circumstances that need to change—it's *us* who need changing.

If God is calling you to stay where you are, how might He want you to "get going"?

....

....

....

....

....

....

....

....

....

....

*Each of us should please our neighbors
for their good, to build them up.*
ROMANS 15:2

It's not automatically better to serve *out there* or *over there*. It's not less godly—or even less brave—to share your faith with a neighbor two doors down than a stranger a world away. It's not more righteous to serve an orphan across the ocean than a foster child across town. All children need love; all these callings—missions near and far—are godly endeavors.

Where has the "spiritual grass" seemed greener to you—another city? A different role? A different job? How can you find contentment and purpose where you are?

....

....

....

....

....

....

....

....

....

....

....

....

....

We continually ask God to fill you with the knowledge of his will through all the wisdom and understanding that the Spirit gives, so that you may live a life worthy of the Lord and please him in every way: bearing fruit in every good work, growing in the knowledge of God, being strengthened with all power according to his glorious might so that you may have great endurance and patience, and giving joyful thanks to the Father, who has qualified you to share in the inheritance of his holy people in the kingdom of light.

COLOSSIANS 1:9–12

God may be calling you to stay home—but staying home doesn't mean staying the same. Even if Jesus is calling you to stay, He is still calling you to move forward: Go deep. Love hard. Grow strong. . . right where you are.

Go deep. Love hard. Grow strong. Which call inspires you the most?

Peter turned and saw that the disciple whom Jesus loved was following them. (This was the one who had leaned back against Jesus at the supper and had said, "Lord, who is going to betray you?") When Peter saw him, he asked, "Lord, what about him?" Jesus answered, "If I want him to remain alive until I return, what is that to you? You must follow me."

John 21:20-22

As tempting as it may be to expend energy worrying about other people's burdens and baggage, comparing them to our own, let us choose to focus on ourselves. On what (and whom!) God has called *us* to bear. To forgive. To become. Just as Peter had to accept Jesus' plans for his life, so we have to accept His plans for ours. Broken and heartbroken as we may feel, comparison does us no good. It steals our contentment, distances us from God and others, and, in the end, changes nothing.

Different as we are, we each are called by God in different ways to different roles—but with the same level of devotion. Different, but the same. *"What is that to you? You must follow Me."*

In what areas is it tempting to compare your burdens with others'? How can you make peace with your burdens, your past, and your current role?

....

....

....

....

....

....

....

....

....

....

*Put on the full armor of God, so that when the day of
evil comes, you may be able to stand your ground,
and after you have done everything, to stand.*
EPHESIANS 6:13

Jesus calls us to use times of peace as times of preparation. In-between times can be in-process times, opportunities to:

- Practice spiritual disciplines that anchor our faith and deepen our convictions.
- Read and memorize scripture so that when Satan attacks, we are armed with an arsenal of scriptures (Luke 4:1–13; Ephesians 6:13–17).
- Fill our faith tank full for days when difficulties drain it.
- Form strong spiritual relationships to see us through painful times.
- Build a prayer life—an intimacy with God—that can weather tough storms.

What one spiritual discipline could you focus on right now (prayer, Bible study, scripture memory, relationships, openness) to help prepare you for future spiritual challenges?

Then he said to the crowd, "If any of you wants to be my follower, you must give up your own way, take up your cross daily, and follow me. If you try to hang on to your life, you will lose it. But if you give up your life for my sake, you will save it. And what do you benefit if you gain the whole world but are yourself lost or destroyed?"

LUKE 9:23-25 NLT

If you keep finding yourself called to sacrifice the same thing, confronted by the same difficulty or weakness, perhaps, as with the rich ruler, Jesus is also looking at you and loving you, but gently saying, "This is your thing. The one thing I still need from you. Stop fighting it, and come follow Me."

What spiritual struggle keeps cropping up in your life? If Jesus were to call you to change one thing today, what would it be?

....

....

....

....

....

....

....

....

....

....

....

....

....

....

"Come," he replied, *"and you will see."*

JOHN 1:39

Sometimes God calls us—or someone we love—to make a sacrifice. And to our human minds, it's too much. The cost is too great. It doesn't make sense. *There's too much suffering in that. That plan doesn't have a happy ending. That can't be the will of God.* And although we don't mean to, we stand in the way of God's call *simply because it's difficult.*

How do you grow differently during times of peace as opposed to times of difficulty?

....

....

....

....

....

....

....

....

....

....

....

....

....

Let the morning bring me word of your unfailing love,
for I have put my trust in you. Show me the way
I should go, for to you I entrust my life.
PSALM 143:8

Even when we can't understand God's ways, we can trust His heart. And that trust—the surety of His unfailing love—brings us peace, rest, contentment.

How has God proven Himself worthy of your trust?

....

....

....

....

....

....

....

....

....

....

....

....

....

....

Then Andrew brought Simon to meet Jesus. Looking intently at Simon, Jesus said, "Your name is Simon, son of John— but you will be called Cephas" (which means "Peter").

JOHN 1:42 NLT

Peter had quite a few of his own come to Jesus moments:

Peter had to (literally) come to Jesus when the Lord said, "Come, follow me. . .and I will send you out to fish for people" (Mark 1:17). Peter had to leave his nets—leave his life—and go wherever Jesus went.

Peter had to come to Jesus after the miraculous catch of fish, a divine display so staggering that Peter cried, "Go away from me, Lord; I am a sinful man!" (see Luke 5:1–11).

Peter had to come to Jesus when the Lord tried to wash his feet but Peter tried to push Him away—again Peter quailed in the face of his own unworthiness. He didn't want the grace (see John 13:1–17).

Peter *should have* come to Jesus in the courtyard of the high priest the night before the crucifixion, but instead he "followed at a distance." And soon he cursed His name (see Luke 22:54–62).

Peter had to come to Jesus—come *back* to Jesus—on the beach after the resurrection, when Jesus gently but pointedly reinstated him (see John 21:15).

Is it time for a "come to Jesus" in a certain area of your life? What is that area, and what is Jesus asking you to do?

....

....

....

....

....

....

....

....

"Come, follow me, and I will show you how to fish for people!"

MARK 1:17 NLT

Peter gives me hope: hope for myself, hope for all of us. Let us learn from Peter that even when we fail—say no, break faith, run away—all is not lost. We have not blown our one and only chance. God can still use us. We can still serve, still lead others *to* Christ and *in* Christ.

Peter proves that when we say no—even the worst kind of no—Jesus is willing to give us another chance. A chance to change. A chance to turn our no into yes. A chance to turn our "But Lord, I—" into "But God can." A chance to go wherever He leads, whenever He calls.

Consider the current challenges in your life. What character traits might God want you to develop through those struggles that could serve His purposes later? How is that growth going—in what ways are you embracing it. . .or fighting it?

....

....

....

....

....

....

....

....

....

....

....

....

> *"Therefore go and make disciples of all nations, baptizing them in the name of the Father and of the Son and of the Holy Spirit, and teaching them to obey everything I have commanded you."*
>
> MATTHEW 28:19-20

When Jesus says, "Come," it's time to go. When Jesus says, "Come," it's time to go big, because when He calls, He wants our all.

What inspires you about "going big" for Jesus?

_____

_____

_____

_____

_____

_____

_____

_____

_____

_____

_____

_____

_____

_____

_____

_____

*"Come to me, all you who are weary
and burdened, and I will give you rest."*

MATTHEW 11:28

Jesus called Peter to go not once, but many times. So with us: "Go and tell. . . . Go and make disciples. . . ." And just as with Peter, so our Lord doesn't only send us out; He also brings us in. Invites us close. For every *go*, there is also a *come*: *Come and see, go and tell. Come and heal, go and share.*

How do you feel Jesus sending you out and drawing you close at the same time? How does sustaining a close connection to Him better prepare you to go out with courage?

....

....

....

....

....

....

....

....

....

....

....

....

....

....

But you are a chosen people, a royal priesthood, a holy nation, God's special possession, that you may declare the praises of him who called you out of darkness into his wonderful light.

1 PETER 2:9

We can take comfort in knowing that God often calls us *because* of our weakness, *because* of our wounds, so that He can redeem them and use them for His glory.

In what ways has God used your weakness for His glory?

....

....

....

....

....

....

....

....

....

....

....

....

....

....

....

When we come to Jesus, when we answer His call—"Tell me to come to you on the water." . . . *"Come!"*—He walks before us and beside us. Even fishes us out of the water when we flounder.

When we come to Jesus, we get to share His joy.

In what ways do you bring Jesus joy?

....

....

....

....

....

....

....

....

....

....

....

....

....

....

....

....

"Come, you who are blessed by my Father; take your inheritance, the kingdom prepared for you since the creation of the world."
Matthew 25:34

We each get our own calls—our own lives, our own burdens, our own blessings. Our own unique ways of walking with Him and serving Him.

But there is one call we all get in the end. Eventually God is going to call and say, "It's time to go home. Time to *come* home. Home to heaven with Me." And that's the call we need to prepare for more than any other.

What do you most look forward to about going home to be with Jesus? What can you do to prepare for that day?

....

....

....

....

....

....

....

....

....

....

....

....

....

....

Let the one who hears say, "Come!" Let the one who
is thirsty come; and let the one who wishes
take the free gift of the water of life.

REVELATION 22:17

No matter what specific roles, responsibilities, and even burdens God hands down to us, we each are called to give our all. To deny ourselves. To put Christ first, before our own desires, before any other relationship. To go with Him wherever He leads. Yes, on to victory, but also on to what the world would call "defeat." To unfairness. To crosses. To sacrifice. To wrongs that are not righted in this world. Even to death that only God will avenge.

How has God used an unfair situation in your life for His purposes and your spiritual growth? Do you find it easier to see God's hand at work in hardship or in victory?

....

....

....

....

....

....

....

....

....

....

....

....

*"Be strong and courageous. Do not be afraid;
do not be discouraged, for the Lord your
God will be with you wherever you go."*

JOSHUA 1:9

Like Peter, let us be brave enough to jump up onto the prow of the boat, lean out over the waves, and shout, "Lord, if it's You, tell me to come."

Then Jesus will turn, flash a proud smile, hold out a hand, and call, "Come!" *Come conquer your fears. Come share My adventure. Come walk with Me.*

And when Jesus says, "Come," there's only one way to respond: we cast fear aside, let go of the rope, and jump overboard, shouting, "I'm coming, Lord! Let's go!"

What do you need to let go of in order to jump out of the boat? Are you ready to go?

....

....

....

....

....

....

....

....

....

....

....

....

Read the book that inspired the journal. . . .

WHEN GOD SAYS "GO"

When God says, "Go," what will you do? Author Elizabeth Laing
Thompson invites you to walk alongside people of the Bible who
were called by God to fulfill His purposes. . .people like Moses,
Esther, Abigail, Jeremiah, Mary, and others. These Bible heroes
responded much like we do—with a jumbled-up inner storm
of excitement and fear, insecurity and hope. Their stories
and struggles will provide a road map for your own story,
helping you face your own doubts, regrets, and worries.
Paperback / 978-1-68322-555-3 / $14.99